What Explains Poverty in India

Chandra Sekhar Gupta Boggarapu

notionpress.com

INDIA • SINGAPORE • MALAYSIA

Notion Press

Old No. 38, New No. 6
McNichols Road, Chetpet
Chennai - 600 031

First published in 2015
Re-published by Notion Press 2018
Copyright © Chandra Sekhar Gupta Boggarapu 2018
All Rights Reserved.

ISBN 978-1-64324-218-7

FOREWORD

A Foreword is a short introduction to the book, usually by a person What explains poverty in India? This is a question every Indian concerned about the country should be asking himself/herself. I know people are not equally capable. I know some perform well and some do not, financially speaking. But the poverty in India that I see is appalling and unjustifiable. I always felt that India and poverty are incompatible. This is very unnatural or put it differently this is man-made. When I started looking at the world around me from this perspective, things started looking different. For very long I did not bother to put my thoughts on paper. But for some reason I have decided to do so now. Again I do not claim that I have written this book for the simple reason that everything mentioned in this book is already known to people, at least the well informed ones.

I just gathered the information already known/available and arranged it in some readable fashion. I did not bother much about the way the content is presented for now since I want to follow it up with improvised editions in quick succession. I look forward to receive inputs from the readers to make the future editions richer in content (like scams yet to be discovered/scams in the making, practical/feasible ideas that can stop exploitation of weak and disadvantaged or anything related to the topic). I shall acknowledge all such inputs publicly.

Let us do our bit.

With very warm regards,

Chandra Sekhar Gupta Boggarapu

P.S. I am neither interested in becoming another armchair analyst nor in sermon giving. I am keenly interested in doing real things in real world. I sincerely urge all readers to send projects/ideas, if any, relating to

- Empowerment of the proletariat/common man.

- Poverty alleviation (through empowerment).

(I am working on some themes that are at planning stage now)

I have started a social initiative under the name 'Proletarian Power' (proletarianpower.org) some time back and I hope to take up the above referred projects under this banner. I would be delighted if you wish to join me in this endeavor. I am also looking forward to work with like-minded people/institutions.

Place: Hyderabad (India)

Date: 27th March, 2015

PERFORMANCE OF 'REPUBLIC OF INDIA' SINCE INDEPENDENCE AT A GLANCE

(NOT based on statistical information but based on popular perception)

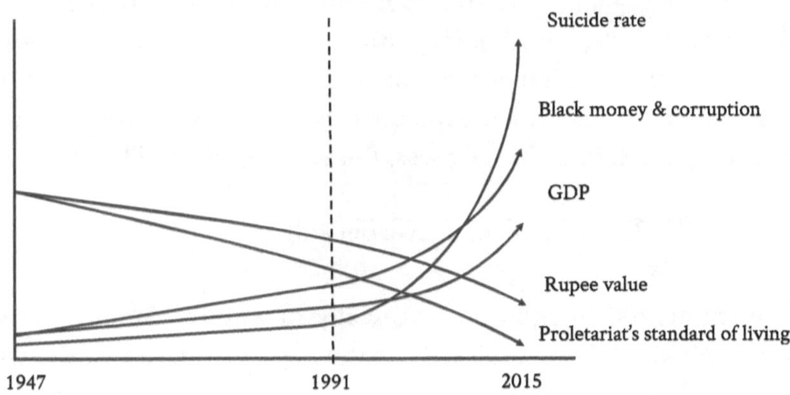

WHAT EXPLAINS POVERTY IN INDIA?

If you think poverty in India is natural, think again. In fact I feel poverty in India is impossible. Yet it exists – it is one big puzzle. India is one of those rare countries in the world that is blessed with all right resources. We have lots of sunshine, abundant supply of sweet/potable water, fertile lands and the last but not the least intelligent and hardworking people. True, all these resources are neither necessary nor sufficient to make a nation prosperous. There are countries which lack most of these resources yet developed and prosperous. India in spite of having all the resources is still a developing country even after 68 years of independence (you can't blame the British anymore). On many social development parameters we are competing with sub-Saharan countries. What explains this status? Honestly I do not have the complete answer, but, I guess, I have some clues. They are:

1.   WEALTH DESTRUCTION BY THE GOVERNMENT

Government(s) in India, intentionally or unintentionally, actively or passively, directly or indirectly, knowingly or unknowingly, willingly or unwillingly destroyed wealth on a massive scale. This process started immediately after our independence and is continuing.

2.   REVERSE ROBIN HOOD SYNDROME

Governments love to play the role, what I call, reverse Robin Hood i.e., 'rob the poor and pay the rich'. There were and are various government policies that have an inbuilt mechanism to make the poor poorer and the rich richer (or transfer the wealth from the poor to the rich).

3.   WRONG ECONOMIC MODEL

Third reasons seems to be blind copying of western model of development (after all most of our leading economists/policymakers are western educated). This model of development is capital intensive, energy intensive, consumption driven (often at the cost of environment) and urban centric. Our policy makers right from the beginning (more aggressively after the so called 1991 liberalization) adopted this model knowing very well that India's capital, energy resources are limited. I believe this model of economic development has pushed us to a status of a perennial beggar (for those evergreen greenbacks).

4.   LACK OF 'AWARENESS' AND 'ENTHUSIASM' ON THE PART OF SOCIETY

Indian society, even the educated lot, does not have awareness about what is happening around them nor has enthusiasm to participate in the process called 'democracy'. Due to such lack of awareness and enthusiasm, over decades democracy in India has degenerated into a single point agenda of winning elections by hook or crook with its own consequences.

5.   DIMINISHED SELF-RESPECT

If I am allowed to go on a slightly philosophical tangent, I feel, somewhere somehow we the Indians as a nation, as a community have lost self-respect (at least partly). A society that lacks self- respect cannot prosper.

6.   FAILURE OF INTELLECTUALS

In any society the intellectuals have a sworn responsibility to fight injustice, to fight for public welfare and common good. On the contrary, in India, most intellectuals either left India for greener pastures or joined the ranks and files of 'exploiters' or still worse, became shoe shine boys of the exploiters. (A few with strong reactive attitude joined extremist/revolutionary groups like naxals).

Of course the above list is not an exhaustive one. For the sake of brevity I would say, the above points give an indication about where we might have gone wrong.

BUT IS THERE A WAY OUT?

Well, we should find 'a way out'. We should find 'a way out' if we wish to leave behind a just, fair and better society for our children.

Then how to solve this man made, complex problem causing great suffering to the vast majority of our population? I believe there are both macro and micro strategies that can be effectively used/deployed to tackle the problem on hand. Before we go into firefighting mode let me tell you a story, well, it is my story.

MY STORY BEGINS HERE

About 30 years ago, after becoming a 'qualified accountant', I entered the corporate world as an officer in (what I call) Corporate Finance Cell of a company. This company was to set up a major cement plant in a mineral rich part of South India. When I joined the company, the project works were about to start. Next three and a half years I worked with this company. During these years I have seen how corporate world function, like the Financial Institutions, Commercial Banks, different government agencies like DGTD (since ceased to exist – thank god). Nothing romantic to talk about. But one crucial observation I made during my first job was that by the end of completion of the project the promoters already earned substantial money (quite a lot indeed). Which effectively means the promoters made this profit by implementing the project (even before commencing commercial operations) and got the project free/without any investment. As a consequence lenders (development financial institutions and commercial banks) and public shareholders are left with a potential lemon. Usually promoter's interest thereafter is limited to exploring the possibility of making more money while running the unit – that is if the unit survives. This is technically known as 'project padding'. Incidentally project padding has a more toxic cousin called 'gold plating'. Gold plating takes place when government(s)/babus fix a price of a product or service based on project cost. Since greater the project cost bigger the returns, the promoters used to pad their projects heavily (thus earning the name 'gold plating') and make sweet returns both by setting up the project and by running it. These projects are absolutely risk free (for the promoters) since either government buys the entire product/service or guarantees the return. In the beginning fertilizers plants were accused of resorting to this mischief. Later when power generation was permitted in the private sector, promoters of these industries too were accused of making a killing like fertiliser plant owners (Crude Oil/Natural Gas exploration seems to be the latest addition to this list). Looking all this I was very excited – honestly. I thought making money in corporate world is simple and fast. But pretty soon I realised that it is not as easy as it appears. One need to be rich, influential and powerful (RIP in short) and well-connected. I am talking about Licence Raj days. Of course things haven't changed much now either. Very soon after making few trips to different government offices in New Delhi I realised that like three Lions in our national emblem there are three powers that run our country viz., lala (industrialist), babu (bureaucrat) and neta (politician). And there is the fourth invisible lion too, like the one in our national emblem, that is mafia (Wonder why so many politicians have criminal cases pending against them?). I gave up the idea of joining them after realising that entry into this club is not very easy. I had to kill my greed and continue to work. I changed/hopped from company to company and kept working for about 15 years. Different companies, different lines of activity, different promoters but the story was more or less same. It would be unfair on my part if I do not present the promoters' case. According to promoters, India is not a country where fair business risk can be taken. They say that they pay/spend good deal of money up-front in getting licenses/sanctions/clearances etc., without any guarantee whatsoever. Hence the rewards should be rich enough. Take it or leave it, your choice (this brings to my mind how a leading and respected industrial house was forced to give up its private airline project – in 1990s – since, it is believed, they refused to please the political bosses of the day – most promoters do not have such compunctions).

This process continued unabated for decades. After few decades of this loot, the country ran out of all its energies and became anemic and joined ICU ward – remembered India physically airlifting gold to London to borrow money, hold your breath, to manage day to day expenses. Then came the great liberalisation that everybody wants to take credit for (sic). I was working in a power generating company promoted by a State Electricity Board at that time. This company though legally a private company it is a *de facto* government company run by babus. Here I had to work with bureaucrats (IAS included) and had an opportunity to see how government machinery works (the lesser I speak the better). The platonic shift that had happened with liberalisation was opening up of infrastructure for private sector (which was hitherto an exclusive prerogative of government). Then I clearly saw two developments taking place. One: there emerged a more powerful, more lethal ultra RIPs who often have direct access to the highest authority of Republic of India. Two: the usual loot which I have seen in Licence Raj period increased by many folds. No wonder few South India based infrastructure kings in India today were small scale industrialists just about three decades back. One must appreciate their grit, guts, agility, shrewdness and everything (Let us give credit where it is due).

Then the big leap – for the RIPs not for Republic of India – came, according to me, with opening up of forex account. One thing I profusely thank God, for some unknown reason, India did not make Rupee convertible on capital account (Don't tell me about RBI road map). Of course it did not stop the RIPs from doing what they wanted to do completely but this has caused some inconvenience to them.

What is interesting, all through this is the Government of the day actively supported the RIPs by all means. The government ever ready to listen to them and act upon immediately, make money available to them at cheaper rates (at the cost of savers), give them land free – practically (again never mind if few small, faceless farmers/tribals lose their livelihood), tax breaks, cash incentives, one time settlements, corporate debt restructures, viability gap funding, what not. Well I should stop here, otherwise I have a very lengthy list. Why should the government do all this you may ask. To develop the country, of course. (in the process if the 'insiders' develop too, it is accidental).

I think we have reached a stage that there is not much to loot any more, the loot is complete. Consequences are for everyone to see. Extreme poverty and billionaire Indians (in USD terms) coexist in India. Increase of such ultra rich Indians took place along with liberalisation – only blind refuse to see the link. Massive amount of wealth – of the nation, of the people, of the proletariat – handed over to few unscrupulous RIPs. Can we reverse it? I really do not know. Nothing short of a revolution can achieve that and Indians are not known for their revolutionary zeal – except for wearing 'Che Guevara' on their T-Shirts.

I would like to leave 'reversing the trend' to scholars (I definitely do not count myself as one), and like to concentrate on arresting further damage – before these RIPs convert India into a moth eaten useless piece of wood. Let us see how that can be done.

My story ends here – rest assured

DISCLAIMER

My statements about 'project padding'/'gold plating', consequent undue enrichment of some people mentioned above or elsewhere in this book are based on my 'educated guess'/market grapevine and NOT based on 'solid' evidence. Further my comments about corruption, corporate frauds, bureaucratic inefficiencies, collusion between politicians-bureaucrats-businessmen etc., in this book are NOT based on data/information that can withstand legal scrutiny. Readers are requested to use their own judgment before coming to any conclusion.

RECOMMENDED PLAN OF ACTION

(In a way this is a proletariat's wish list)

This trend can be arrested only by working relentlessly for few decades both at macro and micro levels. I give hereunder some of such strategies. I warn at the outset that some of them may look impractical, some of them may look outlandish and yet some other may require thorough refinement. But let us make a beginning somewhere. Now here is the list of recommendations (not necessarily in the order of priority):

1. DIVIDE ALL TAXES INTO TWO CATEGORIES, SAY, GENERAL GOVERNANCE TAXES (GGT) AND SPECIFIC SERVICE TAXES (SST).

GGT is meant to finance basic government functions like maintaining army, salaries of babus, primary education, primary health care etc., These funds should be strictly used for pre- defined basic/primary duties of the government and should never be allowed to be diverted.

On the other hand the SST is something government collects from its citizens for the specific service that is rendered.

This division will result

- In checking transfer of wealth from poor to rich (deliberately or Otherwise)
- Empower the citizens (because to collect SST, the government should render some services and must justify the charges)

Let me tell you an interesting story here. Title of the story is 'When CM becomes CEO'. Is it real or is it a fiction? I don't know. (I would like to leave it to your imagination). The story goes like this:

Once upon a time there existed a very intelligent politician in India (where else), who was energetic, shrewd blah, blah, blah. Often he loved to call himself CEO of the state instead of CM. This guy visualised the potential of Information Technology industry in India very early. Being shrewd, he came up with a plan and implemented it very efficiently. Now, the operative part. He identified a nondescript backward village very close to the state capital and started purchasing lands in the village. The village was backward, lands there were not fertile, villagers were poor and uneducated. When they saw some demand for their 'useless' lands, they were elated. After creating substantial land bank, the CEO of the state started developing the surroundings by pouring large sums of government funds (collected through taxes, borrowals). Created great infrastructure there and offered lands (not his, government's) to big and small IT companies at attractive rates and soon nondescript village transformed into a hub of tech companies a la 'silicon valley' (I know you are very intelligent and there is no need to tell you what happened thereafter).

Ideally it is better to have a publicly declared 'taxation policy' based on some philosophy rather than some arbitrary percentage fixed by the Rulers while preparing/cooking the budget. This is discussed in detail in **Annexure 1.**

2. RATIONALIZE SUBSIDIES/INCENTIVES ETC.,

Some simple changes (not that simple, though) that need to be made immediately are:

- Substitute individual oriented subsidies with community oriented subsidies for both individuals and corporate.
- Encourage investment oriented subsidies and discourage consumption oriented subsidies.
- Encourage subsidies/incentives that create enduring benefit to the receiver (individual or community or corporate).
- Wherever possible adopt 'revolving fund' concept so that former beneficiaries support subsequent beneficiaries.
- Subsidies better be restricted to basic needs rather than to support higher aspirations (unless justified by the circumstances).

- All such schemes should be mandatorily subjected to social/independent audit to review the cost benefit analysis of every scheme. All audit reports should be made available to the public (They are funded by the public and society has every right to know how they are performing).

I know it is not as simple as it may appear. Over the years the 'insiders' have devised and implemented various schemes that are 'win-win' for them though they are publicised/displayed as for the benefit of public. Let us try to understand the above points with the help of few examples.

2 (a) Reimbursement of Healthcare Expenses: This is one of the popular schemes with many state governments, particularly in south. Under this scheme 'eligible' poor are reimbursed medical expenses subject to certain criteria. I understand that each state spends about Rs. 1000 crores on this. I never understood logic behind the scheme (besides getting votes and making money). Misuse of this scheme by ineligible people, dubious hospitals is heard frequently. Most of the treatments that are eligible under this scheme, I am told, are secondary and tertiary in nature, not primary. Government is under obligation to explain to the society what benefit the society is getting out of this expenditure (since society is paying for this). This expenditure will not create any facility of enduring nature and simply vanishes in no time (goes into earth may be right word) with the demise of the beneficiary. Further since this scheme is universal, every one, I mean people in any life stage, are eligible. Even very old man/woman - with no productive value to the society - is also eligible for reimbursement. While my words sound harsh, they are practical. Leave it to NGOs, charitable organisations. We have not reached that level of 'welfare state'. Our primary health centers are dysfunctional. Even referral hospitals are in bad shape and they are starved of funds and necessary infrastructure. Corruption is rampant. Whole government health care system is in one big mess. What explains this love for private hospitals (main beneficiary) while government hospitals/health care system is crumbling. Only explanation that comes to my mind is that the rulers of the day can advertise this scheme to get votes and make money from the health care industry (second biggest industry in the world).

2 (b) Supporting Higher Education: Here government(s) can think of 'revolving fund' concept where in former beneficiaries support latter beneficiaries. Let me explain. I have number of relatives who are medical doctors. They studied in government medical colleges (students under merit/open quota). They progressed very well after completion of graduation and post-graduation. Some of them settled abroad and are doing very well, even by the standards of their adopted countries. I am told that government spends considerable amount on making these doctors. So the government may create a 'revolving fund' (preferably at the institution/college level) to which these well off doctors contribute a small percentage of their earnings each year. I am sure they love to do it if the scheme is transparent, reliable and free from political/bureaucratic interference. Funds thus collected can be used for the development of the institution/college and to meet the expenses of new students. After some time, I won't be surprised if the institution/college does not need any government support, whatsoever. This scheme can be implemented in all IITs too.

2 (c) Subsidies to Corporates: Same is the case with the incentives to corporate. Instead of subsidies and incentives to individual units create better infrastructure (better roads, better railway transport system, better seaports, better availability of power) so that industries can work efficiently and become globally competitive.

The above examples give some idea about how our subsidies/incentives can be redesigned so that they become more effective with lesser funds over a period of time.

3. INTRODUCE 'SUPER PROFITS' TAX

We have been hearing about this for the past few years and government has made some halfhearted attempts to introduce super profits tax. Time has come that the government should take up this seriously for number of reasons. But before we proceed further let us try to understand what is 'super profit'. 'Super profit' is not an absolute figure like Re.1 crore or Rs. 10 crores. (It may be so in individual's case). It should be based on some sound logic like return on capital employed in excess of some benchmark percentage, say, 100%. Just an example. I firmly believe that 'super profits' always have an element of contribution by the society. So taxing such excess profit is like giving a part of it back to the society. This tax is also necessary because of many loopholes in the prevailing income tax system - this acts as a second check. Further I doubt some criminal/mafia elements make huge money in illegal ways and declare the ill gotten money as profit from normal business activity - paying 20%/30% is a small price for them (there are many other ingenious ways to bring such moneys into mainstream, I agree). Thus 'super profits' tax can also act as a security check to some extent.

4.   DO AWAY WITH 'ZERO TAX' INCOMES

It is eminently desirable to do away with this policy of exempting some incomes from income tax totally. (Exceptional cases may be there). Whether it is agricultural income or income from equity investment, total exemption leads to misuse of these routes. So such exemptions, if need to be given, must be subject to some checks and balances and also must be based on sound rationale (instead of pleasing the lobby groups). A case in point is how Mrs. Jayalalithaa, then Chief Minister of Tamil Nadu declared agricultural income from sale of grapes that has attracted satirical comments from her opponents.

5.   STOP SQUEEZING THE SAVERS

I do not know how and when this process of squeezing the savers and subsidising the borrowers has started. Savers in India, as long as I remembered, earned negative (real) interest. This is undesirable and unsustainable with serious socioeconomic consequences in the long run. It effectively shifts wealth from savers, mostly middle class, to the affluent business community. (this may be oversimplification, though). Whether the recent Sharada chit fund scam in West Bengal (under CBI investigation at present) or case of Bhushan Steel bribing chairman of a PSU Bank (as appeared in media recently - Company denied any wrongdoing) are rooted in this distorting 'price of money'. Savers go to risky products to earn more and borrowers resort to unethical means to get that 'cheap money' at any cost. So this must end now. Nothing justifies its continuation.

6.   BRING IN A BALANCE BETWEEN INCOME BASED TAXES & ASSET BASED TAXES

While the government jealously/aggressively taxes incomes in recurring nature, it takes a very lenient view of asset based incomes (read capital appreciation). This style of taxing has always been criticised by intellectual in the field of economics. There is no need for treating capital gains with such kid gloves (not only lower rates but also umpteen exemptions to avoid paying even such lower rates). Most of the exemptions under 'capital gains' head are unnecessary. In fact government may consider taxing capital gains annually on 'mark to market' basis, a concept borrowed from stock market. Not just income/direct taxes, even local taxes take a lenient view of propertied. I pay 'property tax' of Rs. 4000 pa to local body for my self-occupied 900 sft flat while RIPs who own acres of vacant land in the city where I live (valued tens of crores) pay nothing. This is absurd. Why can't the government prescribe **minimum FSI** (along with maximum FSI), calculate property tax notionally and collect it from these people. After all urban property is a precious commodity and should not be allowed to be hoarded (I am against to reintroduction of Urban Land Ceiling Act). This move may bring in more land into the market (since hoarding becomes expensive) leading to fall in prices which makes buying a house more affordable for many.

7.   TIME TO INTRODUCE 'BALANCE SHEET'/'NET WORTH' TAX?

No matter what the government does - like introducing MAT etc.,- RIPs seems to have escape routes designed, developed and implemented by 'experts' to avoid paying taxes. One simple way to tackle this problem may be introducing 'balance sheet'/net worth tax. The concept is very simple, Every year increase, if any, in the balance sheet/net worth is taxed say at the rate of five/ten percent. Income Tax, 'super profits' tax already paid may be reduced from this. Experts may think about this.

8.   TONE UP INTELLIGENCE

This is one area I found government is abysmally poor. Intelligence (information gathering) in the field of economics needs to be toned up urgently. Whether Income Tax Department or Directorate of Revenue Intelligence, Enforcement Directorate or other related agencies have no idea about what is happening. (I read somewhere that intelligence is all about 'getting under the skin' of your target - our babus seems to be nowhere near to it). They often swing into action when an issue becomes a public knowledge (if it does not, it never sees the light of the day). Let me explain this with some of my experiences. Most people might have forgotten Ketan Parekh. I was running a small sub-broker office at that time. I heard of him (and his activities - including the companies he was involved with) more than a year before his name appeared in newspapers. If a guy running a small sub-broker office knows what is happening in the market then where were our 'James Bonds' sleeping, I wonder. Similarly on receiving some unfavourable reports, I withdrew my mother's money from CRB Capital more than a year before Chain Roop Bhansali was arrested (India's leading rating agency downgraded their NCDs from A+ to D overnight - speaks volumes about their professionalism). Another case that come to my mind is Abdul Karim Telgi of fake stamp paper scam fame. This scam, I believe, went on for decades unnoticed/undetected. Similarly Satyam Computers is another case (there were many rumors' about this company for many years in the financial markets before the government agencies got wind of it). These cases speak volumes about efficiency (or lack of it) of our intelligence apparatus. Large quantity of black money in tax havens/abroad also confirm their ineffectiveness.

9.   INDUSTRY NEEDS GOVERNMENT SUPPORT – BIGGEST MYTH

Industrialists/Business communities have very powerful lobby groups. They are very resourceful. They employ extremely talented and intelligent people. They always tell government of the day that they should be supported. Otherwise the country will collapse. They are indeed successful so far. My plain and unbiased view is that government neither need to support them nor create problems to them. Business people never do what is not beneficial to them. Average industrialist is not a Mother Teresa. Serving the society is not their goal. I am not saying government should not work with them proactively. Let us understand this with the help of an example. Let us examine working of two industries in India viz., textiles and information technology. Though I do not have any direct exposure to either of the industries, I have some idea about their working. Government(s) have been giving innumerable benefits to the textile industry (across the value chain) for the past four/five decades. Besides usual investment allowances, backward area incentives, they are given special export related incentive, technology upgrade funding, subvention of interest etc., In spite of taking so much of 'public money' the industry is still not competitive, (While the industry itself is not benefited much, it seems, the industrialists' personal wealth increased many folds). Had the government given that money directly to the poor people instead, many would have moved out of poverty by now. Compare this with information technology industry. I know people would say such comparison is unfair. Yet this is one industry that is not only growing, bringing prosperity to millions of people but also helping India in many ways (by earning precious foreign exchange - which our policy makers squander) got no incentive whatsoever from the government (some benefits are given unsolicited). Actually success of IT industry is an interesting case. We will talk about it a little later.

10. (A) INCREASE TAX BASE

This is linked to my earlier point about 'toning up intelligence'. There are many reports stating that our tax base is very small - compared to what it should be. Main reasons for this are absence of intelligence gathering and high levels of corruption. Some time back out of curiosity I started looking around to find out 'how many people in the city where I live are earning Rs. 10,000 or more per day (net of expenses)? To my surprise there is mind boggling number of people in this club. Few examples (estimates based on discrete enquiry):

- A reputed homeopathic doctor attending more than forty patients per day (collects Rs. 1000 per patient).
- A local jewelery shop that sells 10/11 Kg gold ornaments per day during season (6/7 kg in off season)- this is not a branded listed company.
- A popular sweet shop that has a sales turnover of Rs. 1,00,000 per day.
- A tailor who charges Rs. 1500 for stitching one designer blouse (one month waiting period, I am told).
- A popular mess that sells more than 2500 meals per day (plus side dish sale).
- There are number of specialist medical doctors who cross this mark very comfortably.

The list can go on. I am not sure how much of their earnings are reported genuinely. There are number of trades in cities where people make huge amount of money. Typically they are in unorganised sector, family owned, not corporatized, established 30/40 years back (sometimes second generation), survived ups and downs, taken full advantage of urbanisation and increasing population, built a reputation locally, deals only in cash and never give you a bill. Chasing all such sundry traders is neither possible nor desirable. But there must be a mechanism to capture their income and tax it (steps like making cash dealing inconvenient, taxing assets appropriately etc., -

discussed elsewhere - should make them to comply with tax laws voluntarily).

Another interesting observation I made is in towns which are hubs for agricultural commodities pooling/trading, merchants make huge sums of money. Typically they purchase agricultural commodities from farmers, process them, store/hoard/trade them. I understand that they exploit farmers to the hilt due to some peculiarities of agro commodity nature (local government agencies are accused of helping such exploitation). Again all cash deals only. Some of the big time traders may earn couple of crores a year. It is very unlikely they ever show the entire profit (I would not be surprised if they do not show any at all).

10. (B) RATIONALISE/STREAMLINE INDIRECT TAXES

So far we talked about Income Tax only. There are many other taxes like sales tax, service tax, excise duty etc., which are more poorly administered. I guess there is scope for increasing government revenues many fold from these taxes. I have limited exposure to these tax departments. They are very unprofessional and highly corrupt. The ways these laws are framed make them difficult to implement for many small time businessmen leading to rampant corruption. Business people should pay money to the babus, if they want to live in peace. After paying the babus they do not see any need to pay taxes. That way it is win-win for both business people and babus (loss to the nation notwithstanding). This also makes goods and services costlier (inspite of evading taxes) because the businessmen have to recover both money paid to the 'officials' and get compensated for the time, effort and risk he is taking in this connection. Do you wonder, why not the traders/businessmen pay taxes honestly and live happily? If you think so you must be one of those armchair analysts. Truth is whether you pay taxes or not, you should pay to the 'department'. Some time back a retired CTO told me that even professionally run big corporate houses pay them (in cash or in kind - like hotel bookings, luxury cars for their private jaunts) to be in good books of the 'department'. Today we have multiple indirect taxes (that itself is not a problem) adding up to substantial amount in the final price of goods and services. Government(s), whether they like or not, should simplify, streamline these taxes though this may result in loss to some RIPs.

11. DISCOURAGE USE OF CASH

Related to the above we should discourage use of cash as much as possible. I have written letters to Fin Min, RBI, CBDT etc on different occasions suggesting how cash use can be reduced. In this era of net banking, credit/debit card use why should people use so much cash. This is very, very important not only from the angle of tax compliance, but also from the angle of tackling corruption and addressing the menace of fake currency (believed to be pumped in by Pakistan - some people even claim that its is a joint venture of Pakistan and China). Fake currency circulation is a universal menace. For the uninitiated, US Dollar is one currency that most criminals attempt to fake - without much success. Cash, real or fake, in large quantities is dangerous from security/law-and-order angle too. In my correspondence few suggestions were made to bring down cash use. I never got any response from anyone. (I am neither surprised nor upset).

12. GET RID OF DOLLAR ADDICTION

What is the true value of US Dollar? I do not know. I do not think anybody knows it exactly either. Ever since US has gave up gold standard, it has become some kind of magic money (some may call it fiat money). US has worst possible macroeconomic indicators, yet the world loves to invest in it. Dollar is the most powerful weapon US has (more powerful than its nuclear weapons). It just picks up a piece of paper and stamps the words 'US Fed' on it and then it can buy anything with it across the world, anything. Entire world loves it. So be it. We need not get obsessed with it. I said 'do not get obsessed'.

Since we are part of increasingly integrating world, we may need Dollar too. I cannot understand why our rulers should go around the world begging for dollars.

Can't we live with what we have. I have a feeling somewhere this dollar addiction is hurting us seriously and may hurt us even more in future. Did the world learn any lessons with ASEAN crisis in 1990s? India, like every country in the world (except US) has two accounts INR and Forex. Our forex receipts are mainly due to export of labour - exporting labour physically to Gulf/Middle East or techies working for US, Europe - which is nothing but exporting labour. I am told most of our exports of manufactured goods again are labour intensive (by small and medium scale industries) or agriculture and primary products. Either we are exporting our labour or exporting our country bit by bit. For what? To import Gold, Crude which are essentially what the elite Indians consume. I doubt most of this gold vanishes in thin air once it is imported. I wrote number of letters on different occasions to Fin Min, RBI/CBDT etc., to track and see what is happening to this gold (diamonds/platinum etc., included). I never received any reply - once again I am neither surprised nor upset. One thousand tonnes of gold, that is the quantity India imports each year, is a huge forex out flow. I do not know the value of diamonds, platinum etc., imported by India each year. I do not think anybody knows what happens to these imports precisely. Strangely I can not buy a unit of Mutual Fund without complying KYC norms, but I can buy a tonne of gold without revealing my identity. This is clearly unfair. Coming to crude, we give all kinds of incentives to set up automobile manufacturing units which leads to greater crude import bill. I never understood the logic. We will cover this in detail while discussing government's' industrial policies later. To pay for these unnecessary (I mean beyond our genuine need) imports we enter into questionable agreements with Mauritius, allow funds through Participatory Notes, invite fickle FII monies and beg NRIs for dollar deposits. Remembered India Millenium Deposit and India Resurgent Bonds (we used to call them India Misery Deposit and India Detergent Bonds). Incidentally these are highly leveraged wealthy NRI deposits - courtesy their foreign banks. I also heard people having serious reservations about aggressive 'external commercial borrowings' by our private sector. If experts are to be believed we are becoming more and more vulnerable to sudden forex outflows. Remember clearly, when something like that happen it is the poor who suffer the most for no fault of theirs while the rich can live relatively unaffected. I wonder, is there a better way to manage our forex receipts/payments/reserves. I am desperately looking for some expert to take up this issue and give sane advice to our rulers (Whether encouraging rupee trade wherever possible a better option? - failed rupee/rouble trade during USSR era notwithstanding. Should our forex reserves be more reflective of our external trade?).

13. PRIVATISATION AND PUBLIC PRIVATE PARTNERSHIP (PPP)- BEWARE OF THIS NEW FAD

My observation is 'Privatisation & Public Private Partnership' often leads to 'privatisation of profit and nationalisation of loss'. Reasons for this are many. But mainly due to involvement of politicians and mediocre/corrupt bureaucracy. India invented this concept when it was forced to open up in 1990 - we already covered under what circumstances. Then some Harvard/Cambridge/Oxford educated economists were kind enough to help us with their expertise in different ways. Let me explain this phenomenon through one of my personal experience. In early 1990s, when I was working as chief of finance in a power generating company - a *de facto* government company - private sector was invited to take up setting up power plants. Till then power generation was entirely in public sector with negligible private capacity. As with any other public sector, power generation and distribution (distribution is still with govt) was highly inefficient - low capacity utilisation, high transmission losses, time and cost overruns in implementing the projects, political involvement in fixing tariffs disregarding State Electricity Boards' financial health, unruly unionised labour and many such ills. Then with the entry of private sector (modern day angels) policy makers thought (or acted so) the sector becomes vibrant and free of all ills. What happened later is entirely different. The usual *lala- babu-neta* combined force was on full display. While one Enron was exposed many other had a smooth sail (*desi* ingenuity at play probably). Power purchase agreements were proverbial 'heads I win tails you lose' kind. According to experts plants were heavily gold plated. Though the government/rulers know this possibility with their previous experience in fertilizer sector, they still did the same mistake (or trick) while formulating rules for calculating tariff. Industrialist with close connections with politicians got licences - licence raj version 2.00. Little known industrialists entered the scene and became internationally reputed infrastructure players in a matter of couple of decades while Indian economy became uncompetitive - due to higher tariffs - for long long time to come. Though I know that many changes have taken place like tariff based bidding subsequently, the policies, I believe, still favour private power producers and heavily loaded against consumers. Private sector power generation may be as big a scam as 2G and 'coal' but never attracted the attention of any activist. In setting up power plants, at least in the beginning, promoters got benefited through usual 'project padding' and 'gold plating'. Society/common man has to bear this burden ultimately. I understand that distribution is not genuinely privatised and many ills that existed before privatisation continue to exist - double blow to the consumer. We will leave it here. Conclusion is 'Privatisation & PPP' can be a dangerous route - for the proletariat, if not handled intelligently.

14. FINE-TUNE FDI POLICY

FDI policy should be for the long term benefit of the nation. It should not be merely to attract foreign exchange (dollar addiction). It should be based on sound philosophy and rationale, consistent and transparent with a predefined long term goal. Whereas our FDI policy seems to be either arbitrary or cunningly designed and operated with perfect coordination among policy makers, industrialists (domestic and international), consultants, deal makers etc., (looks like 'licence raj' version 3.0) Let us understand this with the help of an example. Let us take life insurance sector as an example. For long LIC was the sole dispenser of life insurance policies in India (since the nationalisation of life insurance industry in 1950s). Let us not get into efficiency or inefficiency of LIC here. After liberalisation the sector was opened to private players initially with 26% FDI and now its is proposed to increase the FDI to 49%. I never understood the sanctity of these percentages. The primary question is do we need FDI in 'life insurance industry'?. Is it in the public interest? If the answer is 'yes' then allow 100% after due diligence of the applicant. Let IRDA take care of the rest. Neither all foreign players are crooks nor all Indian players are saints. What is the logic behind this increasing FDI in stages except that fat-cat promoters who have already got licenses, established business can sell some stake to foreigners at huge profit. Similar situation seems to be brewing up in multi brand retail trade. Quite a few Indian corporate houses have established multi brand retail outlets though it do not fit into their business philosophy. I believe almost all of them are incurring losses but not closing down. Logic seems to be that as and when the government changes its policy and allows FDI in this sector (industrialist know the government's mind better than you and me) they can offload entire or partial stake and make few thousands of crores - cool. For foreigners, with access to unlimited cheap money (read dollars) price is not an issue at all.

Besides the above I do not know whether government or any of its agency ever made any cost-benefit analysis of FDI. I heard some foreign companies have reaped rich dividends on their Indian investments - nothing wrong in itself but as already said whether such invests were needed in the first place. One foreign entity that comes to my mind is this direct marketing company with strong presence in FMCG, cosmetics, nutritional supplements etc., This company is both admired and despised world over for it policies. It fought legal battles and won everywhere. I believe this company is making tonnes of money in India (mainly through its aggressive and unique/questionable marketing techniques). Now the question is 'do we need these kind of companies? (I do not know who gave them permission to enter and on what terms). I am not against to FDI, I am not supporter of protectionism. I have seen enough ugly consequences of protectionism.

But that does not mean that we should not have any restrictions, not yet at least (not withstanding WTO membership).

15. DEVELOP TOOLS TO PREVENT/CATCH/PUNISH WILLFUL AND CUNNING BANK LOAN DEFAULTERS

Common joke we used to make when I was still working (in corporate sector), 'you can see many sick industries but never a sick industrialist' (I am not talking about small scale industries). Reasons are many. Political interference is well known. I have seen rampant corruption in banking sector (both in development financial institutions and commercial banks). Recent arrest of a PSU Bank chairman in Bhushan Steel case is only tip of iceberg (Company denied any wrongdoing). But this itself do not absolve the bank managements from their responsibility completely. I observed that the banking sector, particularly public sector banks, lack appraisal skills. While assisting a Chartered Accountant, in bank audits few years ago, I have come across even senior managers lacking basic appraisal skills. NPA percentage in public sector banks is close to double digit while the same is in low single digit in private sector banks. This political interference, corruption and lack of professional skills damaging the public sector banks phenomenally.

Industrialists, assisted by razor sharp brains in the form of CFOs, Merchant Bankers, Consultants etc., take full advantage of the situation knowing fully that if things go wrong banks will bail them out in the form of OTS, CDR etc., A promoter in the field of infrastructure who is giving sleepless nights to the bankers (in the form of huge NPAs) even has the audacity of posing to newspapers with his Rolls Royce Limo. Eventually, if necessary, banks are bailed out by the government of India with the 'public money'. A company I worked for swindled banks money and shareholders money to such an extent eventually (long after my departure) the company was closed down by the excise department for non payment of excise duty. The promoters blamed the bad market/economic conditions. Subsequently the company revived with generous help of banks and when market conditions improved, the promoters (I understand from the news) sold the company and made a killing. Cool. Isn't it? This episode is not unique. There are tens of thousands of such cases. Revenues collected from the proletariat in the form of taxes on salt to soap are given away to RIPs. Neither any unscrupulous industrialist or corrupt bureaucrat was ever punished nor government has any solution for this. As already said political interference, corruption and poor skills are at play to the advantage of crook industrialists/businessmen. There are number of things banks can and should do to arrest this trend. A comparison of NPA levels in Public Sector Banks and Private Sector Banks speak volumes about this. (PSBs excuses not withstanding). PSBs need to tone up their appraisal skills, gain not only knowledge about finance, accounts and economics but also develop domain knowledge of different industries/sectors. Each industry/sector has its unique dynamics. They not only should be able to understand what is happening in the industry/sector but also be able to see/visualize the future. When even stock brokers have these kinds of facilities/infrastructure, banks have no excuse for not having them. Forensic audits should be ordered wherever a doubt arises. Fixing responsibility for NPAs should become serious (it is casual now). If the government thinks these are too much to do then it should get out of the banking sector totally. Let us not forget that the government still can impose whatever the conditions it wants to impose, like priority lending, on banks. RBI has ultimate authority over banking sector (so far and they seem to be doing a good job in the given situation). To conclude the government should do whatever that is necessary to stop this transfer of money from poor to rich.

16. DO NOT GET OBSESSED WITH GDP - IT IS JUST A NUMBER

GDP is just a number. Giving too much importance to it is dangerous. It can make one believe, as said in my mother tongue, 'swelling' as 'strength'. Actually I have a long list of recommendations to increase GDP in short, medium and long terms. For example by legalising 'prostitution' I am very sure our GDP can go up by a point or two overnight. For morally disciplined people my suggestion may sound bad-in- taste. (Fortunately I am not one of them - actually I am a very deviant guy, morally speaking). I have many such suggestions but I am stopping here since 'civilised world' may consider them 'vulgar'. We are already seeing result of our obsession with GDP increase. Very small number of people are controlling large amount of national wealth. While 'Republic of India' is in dire straits, number of billionaire Indians in 'Forbes list' is increasing (I am sure the list is not complete because there are number of RIPs who do not disclose their wealth completely - out of humility, I guess). While millions of people in India are homeless, lucky few have palatial bungalows occupying acres of land each (or towers raising tens of floors). Just because the proletariat, the common man is not revolting, the rulers should not think everything is fine with the economy. According to a Spiritual Master from South India Who is involved in social service extensively, particularly in Tamil Nadu, more than fifty percent of people (men and women) are shrinking (skeletal structure) in size due to inadequate food. It is estimated that more than 300 million Indians are postponing their dinner to next day because they don't have resources to buy one tonight. Ironically this is so in spite of 'Indian farmers' producing enough food to feed every single individual in the country-what a shame. I wonder what all these GDP numbers add up to if they can't even ensure enough food to its subjects. (In such a situation where is the country going to get its soldiers from, where is the industry going to get the workers from, how can we increase the farm production? If such a large segment of population is impoverished to such an extent, how can this country ever prosper, I wonder). Incidentally countries with impressive GDP numbers are the ones with serious social problems like suicides, drug abuse, high crime rate etc., Are we trying to catch up with them. We better think afresh.

17. CHANGE THE INDUSTRIAL POLICY FROM 'BIGGER THE BETTER' TO 'SMALLER THE SWEETER'

As already discussed big industries - most of them - thrive on government support. They burn foreign exchange, create few jobs (in terms of investment), pay little taxes, abuse their power by influencing policy making while small and medium industries, due to lack of courage/strength to face the system - most of them - just wilt. I believe Germany, a highly developed country even by European standards, has an industrial model where small and medium scale industries play a vital role. Government need to create an environment (not by giving doles) in which small and medium scale industries thrive. Even now, in spite of hostile environment, they are the ones who are contributing to our foreign exchange earnings and creating employment, I understand.

18. CHANGE THE PROCEDURE FOR APPOINTMENT OF COMPANY AUDITORS

At present companies (read promoters) appoint auditors in their Annual General Meetings. They are supposed to give a report on the company's affairs without 'fear or favour'.

Ridiculous. When the auditor is appointed and paid by the promoters how can he ever be free. Recent development of 'rotation of auditors' is plain hogwash. I know some auditors who go to great lengths to get into the good books of the promoters. (I used to be a member of this august institute - not any more). This should change immediately. Auditors of all companies, at least listed ones and ones exposed to bank finances/public money beyond certain limits, should be appointed by government/C&AG/SEBI through fair, transparent method. (ICAI will oppose this with all its strength). Had this been done long ago most of these 'projects padding' and 'gold plating' and other scams would have been avoided and siphoning off public money would have been checked to a great extent.

19. APPOINT 'SPECIALIST AUDITORS' IN SPECIAL CASES

Further to the above Government/C&AG should appoint specialist auditors (NOT necessarily Chartered Accountants) - in addition to the regular ones - where huge 'public money' is involved - like infrastructure projects - to ensure that nothing against public interest takes place. When I say 'specialist auditor' I mean one with thorough technical/vertical/domain knowledge in the relevant field. All these big ticket scams like 2G, 'Coalgate' etc., are seeing the light of the day because of C&AG. Had there been such special/technical independent auditors were in place many of these scams would have come to the public notice much before. We should be thankful to our constitutional writers who have not only created C&AG position but also made it a 'constitutional authority' to protect it from the 'rulers'. In spite of this, '5 year-at-a-time' rulers (assuming full term) has the audacity to question the working of C&AG, a 'constitutional authority'. I won't be surprised if the RIPs are already working to make sure that an obedient C&AG would be appointed henceforth. While C&AG has discovered these scams, there may be many more scams either the government auditor has missed out or yet to find (One issue that comes to mind is Power Purchase Agreements with Independent Power Producers. I hear/read lot of criticism about them. Why not C&AG made any comments about these PPAs). We better understand that these are not ordinary scams. These scams do more damage to the country than enemy's weapons. Adverse effects of these scams last for decades. For now we have found them. But we may not be lucky every time. Further it is better to prevent such scams than trying to fix them. My suggestion about these specialist auditors is intended to serve this purpose.

20. PROTECT 'WHISTLEBLOWERS'

Do not forget that what has become public knowledge after the scams are discovered by C&AG, are already in the know of hundreds of people - besides actual players like politicians, babus, industrialists involved in them - there must be host of people like key employees of these companies, professional consultants, auditors, lawyers of these companies etc., must be fully aware of what is happening. But it never became public. There is a possibility that some of them might have wanted to inform about these scams while they were still in the making, but might have kept quiet keeping in mind the consequences. Attacks, sometimes fatal ones, of whistleblowers are well known. Rulers seem to have little respect/regard for these whistle blowers who help the nation risking their life and limb. This should change. An elaborate system should be developed to encourage people to come forward and inform the government/concerned authority of any wrongdoing that they know. Such people should be protected in all respects and suitably rewarded.

21. APPOINT EFFICIENT, INDEPENDENT REGULATORS WHEREVER POSSIBLE

Independent Regulators like SEBI are not only bringing in some discipline but also helping government in dealing with issues pertaining to the area of their operation. They seem to be doing reasonably good job notwithstanding criticisms from some quarters (something is better than nothing). Having said that, theses Regulators need to be run by intelligent and competent people. Case in point is Competition Commission of India. CCI has penalised cement industry some time back for rigging up prices by cartelisation. If CCI was efficient it could have visualized this before such thing happened. People familiar with the Cement industry, including yours truly, always know that demand was never a problem for this industry (particularly in South India). However almost everyone was incurring losses (with few exceptions) because the industry was highly fragmented and everybody was expanding/adding capacities. One may wonder if an industrialist is incurring losses why should he add more capacity. Theoretically it makes no sense. But the reality is different. Process called 'project padding' (already explained) enriches the promoter - irrespective of benefits to the company (more projects, more money). The game changer was the entry of 'big boys' - foreign variety. They quickly acquired large capacities, consolidated the fragmented industry and acted as price leaders. Rest is history. An efficient regulator is expected to be watchful and prevent these frauds taking place proactively. Fortunately in this case a counter lobby - construction industry - highlighted the issue and (probably) made the regulator to act. I guess but for this high decibel noise raised by the construction industry (it is not a clean industry either) the fraud of cement producers would have gone unnoticed. Another case in point is CERC revising power tariff (upward) for some power generating companies to compensate the increase in price of imported coal for reasons 'beyond their control'. CERC was criticised by many experts for their arbitrary and one sided award. Obviously CERC did not encourage a public debate. May be a better and balanced solution could have been worked out. As already stated a regulator should be intelligent, efficient, open minded and should be capable of seeing the future in the making.

22. THEORETICAL KNOWLEDGE IS USELESS UNLESS GROUND REALITIES ARE UNDERSTOOD.

I often see experts, both in the government and outside, make policies with little understanding of the realities. These experts are educated/exposed/trained at Oxford/Cambridge/Harvard (I never get tired of repeating these names).

They write elaborate theories on 'poverty' sitting in five star hotels (pool side with cocktail in hand, I guess). Let me explain this. I heard on TV once a reputed economist of Indian origin (settled in US goes without saying) advising the government that it should spend more on education. Theoretically perfect. Education is one of the best investment any nation can make. But having worked as a volunteer in some government schools on behalf of a spiritual organisation and as a member of an 'international club' I had the misfortune of seeing their working first hand. I can say confidently that even the amount the government is spending now is a wastage. There are no children in government schools. The few who actually come, they come for the free midday meal not for education. Teachers are not interested in teaching (they are all very well paid for your information). Pass percentages are in single digits. Even the poorest of poor send their children to 'private convents' often paying hefty fee (which those 'private convents' do not deserve). This is the story of primary education. Now move over to higher education. Government - at least in Andhra Pradesh - spend more than one thousand crores of rupees per year in making engineers and other specialists. I heard that many of them are unemployable after their professional education - funded by the government. Should I need to say more about it. Do our 'expert economist' knows all this. Incidentally this episode also shows us yet another dimension of our democracy - since expenditure on primary education is not very rewarding (read more votes), our netas have designed/created special schemes for the higher education (read 'for students with voting rights'). The ideal policy should have been 'efficient universal primary/secondary education and selective/targeted higher education'. This way we could have made every one literate (illiteracy has huge economic costs) and supported serious/committed/deserving few in fulfilling their aspirations (enriching the nation in the process).

23. TIGHTEN FISCAL RESPONSIBILITY AND BUDGET MANAGEMENT ACT (FRBM)

Though we have promulgated this Act few years ago, it seems, governments are not following it sincerely. Besides there may be a need to tighten it further. It seems to me that the present generation is both consuming the saving of past generations and also consuming the yet to be realised earnings of future generations. Public Sector Undertakings, investments made by past generations, are privatised and proceeds are used to meet day to day expenditure. We are borrowing indiscriminately (we know how to circumvent restrictions) which inevitably has to be serviced by the future generations. This is very unfair. Greed of the present generation should be checked (this, of course, is a bitter pill to swallow). Necessary amendments may be made to the Act in this regard. Another issue connected to this is giving away government/public assets to the corporates on permanent basis. Leasing such public assets for certain period rather than selling them away may be a prudent option.

24. BE ON LOOKOUT FOR 'ECONOMIC BLACK HOLES'

Like 'black holes' in the universe there are black holes in economic world too. These economic black holes may be due to legacy of the old systems or deliberately created by the vested interests. It seems Harshad Mehta (stock market scam fame) and Abdul Karim Telgi (fake stamp paper scam fame) exploited such economic black holes. Another incident that comes to my mind in this regard is issuing Urban Co-op Bank Licenses to all and sundries in Andhra Pradesh during early 2000s. Most of them failed as predicted by experts resulting in huge loss to the general public. Either there are economic black holes ready to be exploited or in the making. Government should be alert and always be on lookout (Are you aware of any such economic black holes?).

25. ALLOW THE SICK PSUS TO DIE (UNLESS THEIR CONTINUED OPERATION IS IN THE PUBLIC INTEREST)

There are number of Public Sector Undertakings incurring losses year after year for decades. Many of them are legacy assets. They are big drain of public money. Their continued operation serves no useful purpose. By closing down one Air India, one HMT, one IFCI India is not going to lose anything (actually it gains). Every 'money burning' PSU should be shut down unless its continued operation is in the public interest. Even in such cases operational efficiency should be increased so as to cut down losses.

Case in point is 'free ambulance' service launched in Andhra Pradesh (popularly known as 108 service because anyone can dial 108 and request an ambulance in emergency). Naturally running this service requires public money (a corporate group funds the service partially, I believe). Few years back I wrote a letter to the authorities/trustees suggesting that whenever the patient/victim is admitted in a corporate/private hospital, the authorities should collect reasonable sum from the beneficiary since the one who could afford expensive treatment at such corporate hospitals need no public support. I never received any response.

26. WHAT IS THE NEED OF PNS AND MAURITIUS DTAA

No self-respecting country would ever allow instruments like Participatory Notes nor enter into questionable contracts like Mauritius Double Taxation Avoidance Agreements. SEBI and IT department may play ball with the government (they have to) on these issues. Many experts/economists argue that India lost more than what it gained through these arrangement. To my mind nothing justify these questionable deals, nothing. You don't send your wife to a brothel if you are running short of money. Do you? If you think what I said is vulgar the acts and deeds of government of India are more vulgar. What moral right do we have to fight 'tax havens' in the international forum on one hand and support a chosen one on the other hand. (Is it another case of our 'dollar addiction'?).

27. PRICE IN ENVIRONMENT

Government/Corporate seems to believe that 'environment is for free'. It is not. I wonder how many of our industries are viable if environmental costs are calculated and collected from them. While calculating environmental costs precisely is difficult one should not assume that 'environment' is free. We keep hearing from time to time how local population (forget about flora and fauna) suffer due to degradation of environment by big corporates. Centuries old water bodies and rivers, our heritage, are degraded/destroyed/disappeared in the last 30/40 years in the name of development. If this destruction is taken into account our GDP may go into negative. Economic development at the cost of environment is unsustainable and insane. Development need to be both balanced and sustainable even if it means developing at slower pace. Planet Earth has enough to meet our need but not our greed - whoever said that, summarises succinctly.

28. BHARAT VS INDIA

I have been hearing for very long (particularly from grass root level activists) that 'India' is unfairly exploiting the resources of 'Bharat' and making it poor. I do not know how far it is true. Government/experts may compile and analyse data to find the truth. If the allegations are indeed true, remedials steps should be taken so that people of 'Bharat' can lead a dignified life without government schemes like MGNRES.

29. STOP COPYING WEST

As already said in the beginning copying western model of economic development - energy intensive, capital intensive, consumption driven, urban centric - is destroying India, albeit slowly. This is the case right from the beginning, from the years of our first Prime Minister Jawaharlal Nehru. In this model of development the proletariat/common - man is used as a cannon fodder to make a selected few filthy rich (intentionally or unintentionally). This development model made some people so rich that unable to spend their riches in normal ways they explore new and innovative methods of spending which are disgusting for normal people (buying 4th, 5th... n'th house in Dubai/London is known to everyone. Many of their 'other' activities are not in public domain) Companies promoted by these people, with liberal help from the government, may not be in pink of health is entirely a different matter.

Having discussed at some length about economy/finance etc., in general let us try to look at some specific industries to get a better understanding about what we are talking and what is actually happening. Let us start with Information Technology.

- **Information Technology Sector:** India now known world over for its information technology industry. Without this industry appearing on the scene around early/mid 1990s what India would have been is unthinkable. This industry provides highly paid jobs to millions of youngsters directly and sustains many more indirectly. Now what do you think is the main reason for this success. I know people have many answers ranging from developments in technology, english speaking youngsters, Indian brain power (really?) etc., I have a different take. The above might have contributed, may be. But what lead to this phenomenal success of IT industry is inability of 'rulers' to understand this industry. They could never make a head or tail of it. There is no raw material, no huge machinery, no license/permit required from the government, no request for government land, no request for support from the government, never asked for any aid/incentive, no import/export license required and no labour unrest. What the hell is this phantom industry, they must have thought. Before they could understand basic features of this industry (with the help of their superior IQ) the industry became too big to 'develop and regulate'. I bet every bureaucrat must be grudging that this industry has not given them any chance to 'Develop & Regulate' it in an 'efficient and orderly' manner. (I understand their grief because I have read thoroughly, now defunct, Industrial Development & Regulation Act as a part of my 'education'). Moral of the story: If the government viz., politicians, babus etc., do not meddle with the business/trade/commerce, industry prosper on its own.

- **Life Insurance Industry:** Now let us move to another very important industry. Life insurance is a noble industry. They are out there to protect ordinary mortals like you and me. They are the saviours of the society. Don't believe me. Look at all those colourful advertisement they release in newspaper/magazines at regular intervals. But strangely they are least interested in insuring your life and most interested in managing your money. Funny! Isn't it? Initially there was a monopoly, Life Insurance Corporation of India. Now, of course, enthusiastic private domestic/foreign players have joined the game to help us (We talked about it earlier while discussing FDI policy). The main job of these large hearted people is to collect your savings - somehow - and hand them over to usual RIPs (directly or indirectly) and make some money in the process, not much they tell us (LIC being a PSU has an additional responsibility of helping the government as and when necessary, for example in meeting disinvestment targets). Raw and crude greed of these people was at full display when ULIPs were launched in early/mid 2000s. The industry looted the gullible investors while government agencies were engaged in 'turf war'. They may claim that they never did anything wrong, technically speaking. But the truth is known to everybody who is 'financially literate'. (One of the aggressive players in this ULIP loot is a highly respected financial wizard, who sits on government committees and gives recommendations on various issues). I know agents who sell policies to poor who neither need them nor understand them. For the poor death is not a problem, life is. These companies let loose the agents through aggressive marketing plans unmindful of good percentage of policies lapsing. Government support them with liberal tax breaks, both for the industry and for policy buyers. Is it a case of protector becoming predator? Should the government do something about it, say, remove all tax breaks for insurance except that part of the premium attributable to mortality charges and may even increase the minimum sum assured amount. Something need to be done urgently since many Indians, even educated ones, are financially illiterate. Insurance companies trap them easily. I also wonder whether presence of LIC is giving extra advantage to the private players? I suspect so. How? For now I have some vague idea. I hope to collect more information before saying something about it in the next edition.

- **Automobile Industry:** Let us now move to another 'important industry' in India. That is auto-mobile industry (cars in particular). Before liberalisation buying humble two wheeler was a distant dream for many Indians. Now even four wheeler is within the reach of many Indians. Is it good or bad? I feel India moved from one bad policy to another bad policy. Government showered benefits on this industry liberally. State governments competed aggressively with each other to attract the attention of the promoters. These industries may have created few thousands of jobs. How much the government(s) gained and how much they have foregone or spent supporting it, directly or indirectly. I have no idea. But with the liberal support of the government these companies could produce cars cheaply. With the cheap money made available to the consumers (with a negative income to the savers) people bought them irrespective of its necessity. Result - ballooning crude import bill putting pressure on our delicately balanced forex reserves (till recently India's rating was 'negative'). Governments are forced to spend thousands of crores of rupees constructing flyovers, expressway and ring roads so that these babies - particularly those monster gas guzzling SUVs - can slide on them unhindered. (Pedestrians have no safe sidewalks is a different matter). Governments that could facilitate production of more cars could not expand the radius of planet earth or at least increase size of India. Result, clogged roads and increasing pollution. In the city where I live every major road is being expanded by paying huge sums of money as compensation to the property owners. But even these expanded roads are unable to accommodate the ever increasing automobile population. Besides financial implications this policy has other negative effects too. Life in cities for the people who use two wheel drive, I mean pedestrians not two wheeler, has become daily adventure. Often I take upto 15/20 Minutes to cross a road (most of the time I use my two wheel drive). I often say machines are becoming meaner, drivers are becoming younger and roads are becoming deadlier (for the proletariat/pedestrian). Who cares? One more interesting observation I made is while City buses are barely full, traffic is jammed with personal vehicles. This is unsustainable for a densely populated country like ours. Pollution is another big problem Pollution levels in our cities is way beyond the levels given out by the WHO with serious health implications mainly for the poor. While the concessions and benefits go to the industry and rich, the proletariat end up supporting these excesses. Nothing new. Let me be abundantly clear that I am not against to any industry. Further I have no prejudice against car owners. I own a four wheeler and I have been driving one for the last thirtyyears.

- **Banking Industry:** This is another interesting industry. Everybody, from stock brokers to traditional money lenders to NRIs to Corporate Consultants to every Industrialist wants to have a Bank in his back pocket. There was a demand for making 'bank licenses' available 'on tap'. If you go by the profitability of private banks even a dimwit understands that owning a bank is highly rewarding. Banks never fail (GTB is a different story). I am trying to gather more information before commenting on this Industry - in the next edition. (Inputs from readers are welcome and they will be acknowledged publicly).

- **There are more Industries** I want to look at like **Pharma** (second biggest industry, after defense, in the world), **Infrastructure** (ports, airports, highways - the nation builders), **Power Generation** (that generates wealth - to the producers), **Textiles** (a perennial sick baby with insatiable appetite for public money), **Real Estate** (that never tell you the 'real' story), **5 Star Hospitals** (Recently a pioneer of this industry who received awards from the government of India for his yeoman service to the nation, got angry with the journalists for calling his hospitals 'five star' instead of 'seven star') and many more. May be in the next edition we will discuss about some of them. Once again, any inputs from readers most welcome.

OTHER AREAS FOR IMPROVEMENT

Now let us move on to other areas outside finance, economics etc., to find answers to our main question - 'what explains poverty in India? And how to tackle it.

1.   IMPROVE QUALITY OF 'DEMOCRACY'

India is a democratic country, technically speaking. But as already stated this has been degenerated to one point agenda of winning elections by whatever means. Every limb of our democracy is in dire straits. There are people who argue that India is not a free country. According to them what happened in 1947 is substitution of English Rulers by deshi rulers. It may be an exaggeration but not completely untrue (the amount of distrust Indians have about their own democratically elected representatives/government is astounding). How can we improve it. Let us see:

2   GET RID OF COLONIAL MINDSET

Queen has gone long ago and Union Jack packed and left the shores of India decades ago. But the mindset of our rulers refuse to change. Policies carefully designed/developed/nurtured by the erstwhile colonial rulers to rule Indian slaves continue to exist even after 70 years of independence. Authority, autocracy without accountability are the hallmarks of this system. It seems that the deshi rulers who filled the vacuum immediately after departure of the British in a hurried manner found it very enjoyable.

Recently when police force was placed under the Governor's control in the city where I live due to certain peculiar circumstances, the rulers aired their displeasure/disappointment publicly. I understand their frustration. Politician without police power is like a snake without fangs. British used this force to subjugate the slaves for centuries. Deshi rulers continued the same since independence shamelessly.

Unless India gets rid of this mindset the country cannot progress genuinely (cosmetic progress is already there for everyone to see).

3.   TIME TO FINE TUNE OUR DEMOCRACY?

The model of democracy that we have copied from the west seems to have resulted in some ugly/undesirable developments. I hear some people saying that this model is suitable for enlightened societies (where average citizen is well educated, well informed and actively participate in this process). Taking advantage of our backwardness and ignorance, all politicians (barring very few exceptions) played murky games to win elections often weakening the very nation they want to rule (sorry, serve). Prime object of every political party seems to be destroying the other parties and grabbing power at any cost - even if it means destroying the country. This is dangerous. We have to devise a democracy that is more suitable to us. I believe solutions are available. The point is the existing system has caused considerable damage to the nation and needs to be refined urgently.

4.   INVEST IN 'HUMAN CAPITAL'

There was a famous writer/freedom fighter by name Gurajada Appa Rao in Andhra Pradesh. One of his famous quotes I heard (translated into english, roughly) is 'nation means people, not land/soil'. This is a very powerful and forceful statement, if one understands it. Where are we after seven decades of independence? The rulers, the leaders, the intellectuals clearly failed in their duty inexcusably. I believe we are at the bottom of 'human development' index competing with sub-Saharan nations. The fear, the anxiety, feeling of insecurity is widespread (even among the well-educated and well placed people). According to a report I read in the newspapers India is becoming suicide capital of the world. I read more than fifteen people are committing suicide every hour. This cannot be called development. Identify the talent, nurture/support it. Encourage innovation. Remove mistrust about the 'rulers' from hearts and minds of people. It is time to rethink, reflect on our policies/philosophies.

5. ENCOURAGE PUBLIC PARTICIPATION

The main difference between dictatorship and democracy is public participation. In a vibrant democracy public should be encouraged to participate in decision making. However in India public participation in governance is practically nil except once in five years voting. Being slaves for many centuries Indians probably are not ready for this new role. On the part of the rulers they like it this way. I see this right from the beginning. Public opinion should be channelised in a structured fashion and taken into consideration while major policy decisions are taken. Government should form/encourage/support institutions/ NGOs to examine every policy from the public interest angle. True, many issues in this globalised economic environment are beyond their comprehension. Experts in some form should step in to help them. This is particularly important because there are powerful lobbies that work for specific groups like the industry. These groups not only have enormous resources at their command but also have direct access to the highest echelons of the government (including cabinet ministers and Prime Minister) In the absence of counter view governments are likely to take wrong decisions (in favour of lobbyists). There should be a transparent mechanism in place through which all stakeholders express their views and vetted/screened by experts and then forwarded to the government. This is a desirable procedure unless the issue on hand is of 'urgent' in nature.

6. STRENGTHEN ALL SEGMENTS OF DEMOCRACY

All parts of our democracy like judiciary, executive, legislature etc., are in poor condition. Without refining and strengthening them India cannot prosper. Let us look at each segment closely:

6. (a) Judiciary: A civilised society stands out from an uncivilised one by the presence of an efficient/effective justice system. Our record on this count is pathetic. Our judiciary is dysfunctional, steeped in corruption, manned by poorly trained people, insensitive to the suffering of the victims. In a way India has become a very dangerous country to live in because the law in India acts selectively (some people say lawlessness is far better). Law here helps only rich and powerful. Ordinary folks lost faith in it. We as a society have accepted this. There are many films in which a don is shown running a 'private court'. Nobody find it odd because it is a reality for many, I believe. Theoretically speaking one can go to court and get justice. But then it is only theory. Reality is different. Probably rulers like it this way - for obvious reasons. Effective, efficient and transparent justice system is prerequisite both for faster development of the nation and general well being of the people. This is the most import infrastructure any country should build first. Airports, expressways, power plants can wait.

6. (b) Bureaucracy: Bureaucrats come in different shapes, sizes and colours, figuratively speaking. Starting from not so humble 'chaprasi' to commissioners, directors-general, secretaries etc., there is a full range of them. They may be IAS or Engineers or plain graduates (holding high position because they have sufficiently aged). I had the misfortune of seeing our bureaucracy from very close quarters for few years. What is common to all bureaucrats, according to my observation, is that they all have 'small brain' and 'big ego' (there may be some exceptions). They all think 'we are the rulers' and 'we know everything'. They often go to great lengths to justify their existence by creating trouble to people. Many times they act like 'sand in the bearing'. 'Red tape' is a term the society identifies them with.

Let me explain this with an example. I have a house in a south Indian city in an approved layout. When I tried to sell this sometime back I am told that it needs a clearance from the Commissioner of Urban Land Ceiling. I was surprised and checked up with the concerned office through some known 'contacts'. I am told that out of about 25 acres of lay out a small portion of land in one of the survey numbers require clearance. The commissioner has put the entire 25 acres within the ceiling purview. This is a very cunning ploy. Now everyone in the colony has to visit this office and get a clearance - after 'satisfying' the officials there. I understood from a reliable source that there are hundreds of colonies/lay-outs forcefully brought into their 'grip' in this manner. Incidentally this amply demonstrates' power without accountability' the bureaucrats enjoy.

There is no point in blaming individuals. Whole system need a overhaul. Rulers, particularly bureaucrats, should be made aware - may be as part of their training - that they are not appointed to rule the people but to serve the people. While elected representatives come and go every five years these are the people hang around till superannuation. I think selection methods, training methods and even their designations, everything should be changed. ('Bureaucracy in India' is a serious subject itself. It is worth writing a book about, if nobody has written it yet). I read somewhere that there used to be a tradition in India that a King-to-be is made to make a living by begging for certain period of time before coronation. What better way to make a king humble. It is the time to rediscover ourselves as a nation, as a nation that is both humble and confident, as a nation where rulers value people. With the present set up that is near impossible.

6. (c) Legislature: There is nothing I need to talk about. Use of muscle power, money power is rampant in our elections. People with questionable background are becoming elected representatives. In a way, over a period of time, this has evolved into a system where good people just cannot survive. Part of the blame lies with the people too. As already said effective and efficient judiciary could have checked this menace to some extent. Bringing in some kind of check on 'freebies in the form of election promises' is an urgent need. Pockets of influence like creation of slums should be tackled.

Let me share with you an interesting story here. In a south Indian city there was a famous politician whose modus operandi to create a loyal voter base was 'occupy government lands and create a slum' on it. (India has slums not because of poverty but because our politicians love them). For very long, concerned authorities were watching this helplessly. Then they came up with a brilliant idea (something very rare) and started tracking his 'create-a-slum-

build-a-vote-bank' projects closely and started pre-empting his plans by developing/converting all such urban lands into public parks. How do you like this?

We need to develop a unique system taking into consideration peculiarities our society has. What works in US or Great Britain may not work for us. We are very different from them in many ways. Some of the points that come to mind are:

- Making registered political parties more organized.
- Restricting/discouraging entry of independent candidates.
- Prescribing minimum gap between two 'no confidence' motions.
- Checking the ills of 'outside' support etc.,
- Government may also think about funding elections, with checks & balances, to encourage good people to enter politics.

6. (d) Press: I have been listening very disturbing trends in the field of press, an institution once highly respected. Politicians, businessmen and press collusion seem to be a new game - like particular publisher supporting/condemning particular party or particular leader. Now politicians/businessmen started controlling press - through their own ventures. Recently a key executive of one well known TV channel was arrested for trying to extort money from a businessman, who is also happened to be an MP. I understand that situation in vernacular print media and parts of digital media is very bad. I do not have any further comments for now.

7.   USE TECHNOLOGY

Compared to 20/30 years back, today we have excellent high tech tools that can be used innovatively to improve governance. Though the government started using them in some areas, the pace and extent is disappointing. Deploying such tools not only check menaces like corruption, red tape but also improves government's efficiency and saves substantial expenditure. I have seen government institutions/departments that have streamlined procedures using technology resulting in both reduction in corruption and better service to the public. We can not expect this to happen in the government departments on their self initiation. (since they have vested interest in continuing the old corrupt systems). It should come from outside. Government should chart out a mechanism by which each and every department should function in an environment driven by tamperproof tech platform that minimises public interaction with the babus, remove all discretionary powers - a source of corruption, keep track of their working etc., Since India is a country that provides tech solutions to the world we should not have any problem in this regard.

8. GOVERNMENT SHOULD BITE WHAT IT CAN CHEW

As the old idiom says biting more than what you can chew is not a wise thing. Governments in India are fond of biting everything making the life for the general public miserable in the process. This craving for power and urge to be master of everything is one of the main reasons for corruption that people face every day. This attitude of the government also makes every system imperfect, inefficient and expensive. Common man is condemned to bear the brunt of this government excesses. Government should give up its role of controlling everything and instead concentrate on developing sophisticated systems with checks and balances. Whether it is constructing a building (even a hut if you want to have a registration number) or operating a hotel (even if it is a road side tea stall) everything needs a 'permission' from the 'competent authority'. Is it possible for the government to do everything? In spite of volumes of rule books and army of babus things are not in order.

This brings to my mind Building Regularisation Scheme (BRS) launched in Andhra Pradesh few years back. Without going into the details, the State Government suddenly woke up and found that many buildings in Hyderabad/Secunderabad are constructed in violation of Government Rules/Sanctions. Out of compassion the government has given an opportunity to erring citizenry to pay some penalty and seek condonation. State Government collected about Rs. 1000 crores from penalties under this scheme

(Babus, Civil Engineers/Architects, Consultants/Brokers etc., are believed to have made couple of thousands of crores). The joke in circulation then was except 'clock tower' - a British era landmark and Assembly building - a Nizam era construction, every other construction violated 'rules'. **It simply means Government made rules that are either impossible to follow or impossible to implement or both.** *This is exactly what bureaucrats love- don't ask me why.*

Governments should learn to prioritise issues and should learn doing things in a least disruptive/disorderly manner. If constructing a building is such a hassle free operation in US or Canada why can't it be same here? Incidentally no bureaucrat was ever punished for failing to implement government rules in the above case (putting differently, for looking the other way when constructions in violation of rules were taking place).

9.   CHANGE THE MODE OF GOVERNANCE

Connected to the above government should withdraw, wherever possible, from performing things by shifting from 'doer' mode to facilitator/enabler/supporter/arbitrator mode. Governments should refrain the temptation of actually doing things (which in any case they are not good at). Instead government should play the role of facilitator. This change of mode may also result in reduction of manpower requirement (read downsizing the government) with its own benefits, both to the government and to the society at large.

10. CONTROL CORRUPTION

Corruption is not about somebody getting rich illegitimately. It can make a nation incompetent. Most people consider corruption as mother of all ills. But there is no country that is free from this evil completely. Though this is a dangerous disease I generally do not like to call 'corruption' as a menace. It is a symptom. You can't treat a symptom without attending to the disease. The disease is imperfect system. Improve the systems, make them perfect (as much as), corruption automatically comes down. While businessmen often complain about corruption, I think, they actually like it. One, they always pass on the cost of corruption to the ultimate consumer and thus they are not the losers. Two, for every one rupee they pay in bribes they gain two rupees. Effects of corruption are discussed in detail separately in **Annexure 2**.

11. PROFESSIONALISE THE BUREAUCRACY

When I joined this 'de facto' government company as head of finance, I was amused with everything and everyone around. Being a company (incorporated under the Companies Act) promoted by a State Electricity Board. I as an employee of the company had to interact with employees of the Board at all levels. It used to look like a big circus to me. Having worked in private sector for almost a decade before that my idea of an organisation was entirely different. One striking difference was absence of professionally qualified people, particularly in Finance Department (most striking to me because that was my specialisation then). Finance is least important function for government, diametrically opposite to private sector (You know now why government finances are in such a mess). HR in government is namesake, administration - free for all, marketing - unheard of, and so on (To be honest it was hilarious and very entertaining). Governments could run, albeit erratically, with all these imperfections when India was a closed economy. With India opening up, private sector deploying highly qualified and intelligent people, governments are bound to lose unless they tone up quality of their bureaucracy.

12. CUT DOWN HOLIDAYS AND INCREASE WORKING HOURS

In this 'de facto' government company one major difference I acutely felt on the very first day (a pleasant one indeed) was reduced working hours. In private sector employees work for 8 hours a day (actually people work 10/12 hours). But babus work (don't laugh) only 6 hours a day. Why this privilege given to them is beyond my comprehension.

Further all central government offices work only for 5 days (with extended hours to make up the total prescribed working hours per week). This is how the developed world works, one may argue. But we are neither developed country nor work like them. It is another instance of aping the west. Another observation I made while working in this company was babus can plan it in such a way that they need not work (again don't laugh please) more than 200 days a year. There are plethora of leaves, holidays, optional holidays so on so forth. Many times babus club these leaves and holidays/week ends in such a way that whole government comes to a grind halt for as long as one week. This issue need to be looked at. A cynic may argue what difference does it make to have them in the office for longer hours and on more days. That need to be attended separately.

13. CREATE INCOME GENERATING AVENUES IN RURAL AREAS AND ARREST MIGRATION TO CITIES

I believe that there are number of ways income of rural people can be increased. In other words there are many ways by which additional streams of income can be created to the rural poor. Our 'rulers' who are all ears to those rich and influential neither have interest nor time to think about them. (Bureaucrats who always compete for plump posts in best location with attendant perquisites have least interest in such things). Few schemes that are designed in this regard are not very successful due to their faulty implementation, I believe. Another important point that I may mention in this connection is our new found love for 'urbanisation'. Recent news suggest that Government of India wants to develop 100 'Smart Cities' and Finance Minister has allocated Rs. 7000 crores for this. One of our central ministers recently said urbanisation is taking place because people want to live in cities to improve their standard of living. It may be partly true but many are moving to cities because they are unable to survive in villages. I bet substantial population living in those urban slums would love to go back to their villages if only they can make a decent living there. Further our rulers should know that cities are costly to make and costlier to manage. Cities are extremely energy intensive and highly eco- unfriendly (smart or dumb). They attract intellectuals and criminals alike. Urbanisation is like a double edged sword. It need to be handled carefully/deftly. Do our rulers have that skill? Records so far are not very positive.

14.   ATTEND TO AGRI SECTOR

What is wrong with our agri sector? I don't know. Honestly my knowledge about agriculture is nil. My intelligent ancestors moved out of this mine field long ago. Everything seems to be wrong with this sector. Tens of thousands of farmers committing suicide each year. They are toiling throughout the year yet barely get enough to sustain a modest/decent living. Ironically consumers find prices of agri goods unaffordable. Lakhs of tons of food grain is rotting in government godowns. Yet rulers neither have solutions for nor time to think about millions of these 'unfortunate souls'. Billions of dollars, US Dollars, are spent by Government of India and different state governments on various irrigation schemes, apparently with no commensurate and tangible benefits to the nation (another case of siphoning off public money from the system by the RIPs? - are you hearing C&AG?).

15.   EMPOWER THE PROLETARIAT/THE COMMON MAN

Education and empowerment of proletariat make a country strong, I believe. But our rulers, instead, like to make them dependent on the government eternally by giving them various kinds of doles/freebies which are actually fictitious/artificial. (case in point is 'one rupee per kg rice scheme' - discussed in detail in Annexure 3).One way governments can empower the society at large is by providing minimum basic facilities at affordable price. Put it differently, by removing insecurity feeling (for survival) from their minds. Basic physical, emotional needs of the general public should be brought within their reach (not free - except for destitute). However recent development in the fields like 'primary education', 'primary health care' are disappointing.

Government should also be given respect where it is due. One instance that comes to mind in this context is 'Right to Information Act'. RTI Act might have made lives of many babus miserable but it has given a weapon to the common man that is far more powerful than AK47. Hats off to the one who has proposed this law - knowingly or unknowingly. Another instance of empowering the disadvantaged that comes to my mind is opening of 'rytu bazaars' (farmer's market) in Andhra Pradesh. Farmers, particularly the ones growing perishable commodities like vegetables (mostly small farmers) were exploited by the unscrupulous middlemen for long time. When government opened special markets for them in urban centers these farmers (to some extent) are freed from the exploiters and consumers benefited from lower prices. Governments should look at more such programmes that support vulnerable segments of the society.

16.   KEEP AN EYE ON POPULATION GROWTH

When I was in college people used to talk about population growth as one of the biggest problems. Policy makers used to say that whatever the country achieves is nullified by the growth in population (That was the time when the government used to pursue 'family planning' aggressively). However of late this seems to be diminished in importance. Probably economic growth, real or induced, may have created opportunities for growing population (quality and sustainability of these opportunities is debateable). Recent reports suggest that India's population should stabilise by 2020. Inspite of all these developments government should not ignore this problem, I guess.

17.   DEVELOP SELF-RESPECT

I have this strange feeling that India, as a nation, as a society, lost self-respect - at least partly - for the reasons not understood by me clearly. It may be due to prolonged rule by foreigners. Tens of thousands of farmers dying each year yet society does not bother about them. Millions of Indians migrate to Gulf/Middle East and work in most inhuman conditions, taking risk to their life and limb, just to make a living - helping India in the process - yet the society hardly take note of them. We worship all and sundry but ignore real achievers.

Permit me to tell you one interesting observation here. There is a busy traffic junction in the city where I live. Speciality of this junction, in a way, is there are two statues, one for a political leader and another for great engineer and proud son of India Sir M.Visvesvaraya. While I do not know much about achievements of this political leader I am sure everybody knows about achievements of Sir Visvesvaraya. Every time I pass by that junction (particularly during nights) I observe that statue of the political leader is well maintained and illuminated but the statue of Sir Visvesvaraya is ignored.

If we do not have self respect, we can not expect anyone to respect us. A society/nation that has no self respect can never progress.

18. TIME TO REFASHION OUR RELATIONSHIP WITH OTHER COUNTRIES?

I know nothing about politics, much less international politics. Still I would like to say few words (please forgive me for this):

- **Pakistan:** Peace with Pakistan is impossible, I think. This is not an emotional outburst but based on my assessment. Kashmir, Siachen etc., are excuses. India should understand, appreciate and accept this and develop its philosophy/strategy accordingly.
- **China:** China is an emerging 'superpower'. This is not a good news, neither to India nor to the world (China never hesitated to teach a lesson or two to its Asian neighbours when they defied its authority). For decades China played its cards intelligently by propping up Pakistan against India to tie it down and to wear it out. China succeeded in this game phenomenally with least costs. China is unlikely to change this policy anytime soon.

- **Russia**: Russia, successor of USSR, cornered by the west, particularly by US, will be forced to align with China irrespective of its liking or disliking.
- **Europe and US:** Aging/fading/declining yet potent power (for now) living off colonial era riches (read loot), post war industrialisation dividends and black money stashed away by crooks from third world economies. Confused, bruised and out of touch with ground realities. (The day world discovers alternate system, not necessarily alternate currency, to the Dollar - which eventually has to happen - this block lose its power rapidly, I guess. This may be closer than we think).

Whoever is going to rule India and whatever may be their political ideology, their hands are going to be full in balancing ever hostile Pakistan, aggressive China, unreliable/opportunistic/cunning West. It goes without saying that India needs to become strong from within if it has to face this world reality. Otherwise - no, I do not want to think. One can make India strong from within by ensuring peace, prosperity and justice for every Indian (I mean, including the proletariat), by not treating them as slaves. There is no other way.

Good luck, India.

Tail Piece: When I see the RIPs becoming bigger and stronger by the day, I can not help but think of cancer cells. I believe 'cancer cells' become bigger and bigger at the cost of their host and eventually kill their very own host and die along. What do the RIPs think? They can migrate to a safer place. Is it that simple?

ANNEXURE 1: TAXATION PHILOSOPHY

In the beginning I said the government/country better have a taxation policy/philosophy. What can form basis for this. Let us see.

- When it comes to Direct Taxes, the government should leave enough in the hands of individuals to maintain a decent living (besides *roti, kapda, makan few other things like education, healthcare etc.,*) - no conditions please.
- When it comes to indirect taxes, the government should clearly have a minimum and maximum percentages. Particularly government taxes as a percentage of ultimate retail price should not breach a pre-prescribed limit.(say 20%). Let us not forget that indirect taxes do not discriminate between poor and rich. That way they are ruthless. But again under 'specific service tax' regime - discussed earlier - government can mop up required funds without burdening public in general.
- There should be in place 'super profit tax'. This is already discussed.
- Taxes should be divided into General Government Taxes and Specific Service Taxes. This is also already discussed.
- Government's inefficiency in managing its finances should not be used as an excuse to increase tax rates. Can you ever fill a sieve by pouring more water into it?
- Taxes should not be disruptive in nature. Various taxes in India are designed and implemented with one prime motive of mobilising resources for the government. While governments do need funds to run the government, such revenue collection should not be disruptive thereby increasing cost of goods and services. Very often corruption in the bureaucracy is result of

these disruptive, complex, difficult to follow, one sided laws (lack of accountability make this game lot of fun - for bureaucrats). Because of this faulty methodology society spends Rs. 500 while government collects Rs. 100.

- Taxes should be simple, uniform, non-discriminatory, non-arbitrary, based on sound logic, free from bureaucratic/political meddling.

ANNEXURE 2: CHARACTERISTICS OF CORRUPTION

- **Corruption is one of the greatest destroyer of the wealth** (I mean wealth that belong to the society): Look at billions of dollars of money stashed away in foreign banks/tax havens that belongs to the society. No wonder high levels of corruption and extreme poverty always co-exist.

- **Corruption always flows downwards:** If you ever come across a corrupt officer, know that his/her superior is corrupt too. It is extremely difficult to be corrupt when the superior is strict and straightforward. In fact in many cases of corruption I have come across it actually starts at higher level and then the people working below get embolden to indulge in corrupt practices. So the process of cleaning should always start from top (India has a huge problem here. Number of Ministers, Chief Ministers and a Prime Minister, Chief Secretaries faced/facing corruption charges).

- **Corruption distorts resource allocation to the detriment of 'public interest' and demands reduction in standard of living:**In corrupt environment resource allocation, natural or otherwise, benefit few individuals/corporates at the cost of general public. Over a period of time it leads to concentration of economic power in the hands of few individuals and consequently vast majority suffer reduced standard of living which ultimately lead to social unrest or even a civil war in extreme cases.

- **Corruption is universal:** Know that there is no country that is absolutely free from this disease. It exists, I guess, as long as humans are not free from greed. That does not mean we should accept corruption passively and carry on. It can be managed at levels that do not challenge nation's economic growth in a sustainable and equitable way.

- **Corruption more often than not is a result of wrong/imperfect system:** Corruption always takes place when we have a wrong/imperfect system. Such system might have been devised by some vested interests in the first place or it may be an accidental development or a result of wrong philosophy. All that the government needs to do is correct the system. (Unfortunately often an imperfect/defective system suits the powers that run the government). This is exactly where social activists/NGOs should work seriously. Punishing the corrupt is must but preventing corruption is best and this can be achieved only through improving the systems.

- **There is nothing like 'good corruption':** I heard people saying some forms of corruption, like 'greasing the palm' etc., is actually good since this form of corruption motivates babus work fast. Whoever says so must be a crook who got benefited out of such practice. There is no good corruption or low level corruption. Corruption is bad. Period.

- **Corruption increases the cost of doing business (making the society/nation less competitive):** Corruption can make a society/nation incompetent (There are many other factors that can influence competitiveness of a society/nation and this is one).

- **Corruption demoralises and pollutes organisational environment:** I have seen 'babus' who do not get an opportunity to make that 'extra money' (while somebody is) hardly interested in doing their work. I have seen a few becoming mildly mentally sick too. (Public perception may be that all bureaucrats make money. But the truth is only lucky/chosen/well-connected few get such opportunities - again this varies from department to department).

- **Remuneration and corruption:** I heard some people saying that increasing remuneration will reduce corruption. But the link, if any, between corruption and remuneration is very weak. In any case at present, after fifth pay commission and subsequent revisions, bureaucrats are one of the best paid employee category in India.

- **Spiritual angle**: I heard two enlightened masters talking about corruption. They are given hereunder:

    a) "You don't take bribe from your own people, your parents or spouse or children etc., It is the lack of 'sense of belongingness' that makes one corrupt."

    b) "...I met many people. They are not complaining about corruption. Their only complaint is that they are on the wrong side of the corruption (laughs) Power do not corrupt people.

    People are corrupt. When they get empowered, it becomes apparent."

ANNEXURE 3: 'KILOGRAM OF RICE PER ONE RUPEE' SCHEME

This is the most popular subsidy scheme every politician of India, repeat every politician, loves. The scheme is:

Supplying one kilogram of rice at Re.1 (rupee one, you read it correct) to *poor people.* The scheme says all poor people will get rice practically free (since Re.1 ceased to be of any value long ago). The scheme (and its variants) proved time and again in winning elections. Besides winning elections, this scheme, I believe, is a milch cow (or money cow) to politicians, traders and babus and to many other intermediaries. In brief, under this scheme, government takes/impounds certain percentage of rice from millers at some 'prescribed rate' and then channelise such rice through (leaky) public Distribution System to the eligible poor for Re.1 per kg, upto 5 kg per head per month. While this is the scheme that appears on paper, it actually works very differently. Now let us see that too:

- In a south Indian state the eligible poor people are more than entire population of the state. So there are many invisible poor (only politicians can see them)
- The rice is mixed with foreign bodies like stones etc enroute (rice to that extent goes out the system is obvious)
- I believe almost half of such rice leaks at various points.
- Substantial quantity of such leaked rice goes back to the rice miller at a price substantially lower than that at which they sold it to the government in the first instance.
- This recycled rice is sold to the government by the rice miller again (at huge profit goes without saying)
- Many times poor who receive this rice find it substandard and unfit for consumption. So they sell it in the market, I heard, at Rs. 10/12 per kg.

- Poor are not benefited since 5 kg per month per head is not sufficient to them (assuming that they actually get and consume the rice). So they have to buy rice, another 5/6 kg per head, from open market at higher prices (higher prices, may be due to this scheme - somebody has to pay for the leakages in the system)
- Babus demand and get their pound of flesh/profit for allowing this con game to take place smoothly

Thus it benefits none but RIPs. This scheme is a win-win-win for politicians, traders, babus and all the intermediaries along the path. I believe, price of rice in open market - across all varieties - shot up due to this scheme paradoxically hurting the poor most. Occasionally genuine poor do get good rice but only occasionally. This scheme is particularly popular with politicians, I believe, because it gets them votes, money, name/fame besides rewarding their loyal supporters. There are number of such schemes designed for the benefit of the poor and end up benefiting the 'insiders'.

NOTES